The Powerhouse

An all-in-one resource for building
self-esteem in primary schools

Programme devised by

Elizabeth Morris & **Katie Morris**

Illustrated by **Philippa Drakeford**

How to use the CD-ROM

The CD-ROM contains a PDF file labelled 'Worksheets.pdf' which contains worksheets for each session in this resource. You will need Acrobat Reader version 3 or higher to view and print these pages.

The document is set up to print to A4 but you can enlarge the pages to A3 by increasing the output percentage at the point of printing using the page set-up settings for your printer.

To photocopy the worksheets directly from this book, set your photocopier to enlarge by 125% and align the edge of the page to be copied against the leading edge of the the copier glass (usually indicated by an arrow).

ISBN: 1 873 942 74 5

Published by Lucky Duck Publishing Ltd.

www.luckyduck.co.uk

Commissioned and edited by George Robinson
Designed by Helen Weller and Wendy Ogden
Illustrated by: Philippa Drakeford
Proofread by Sara Perraton

Printed in by Antony Rowe Limited

Reprinted February 2004

Contents

School of Emotional Literacy

The School of Emotional Literacy was created to provide on-going professional training in emotional literacy development. It also allows specialists in emotional literacy assessment and development to give consultancy and training to schools, LEAs, social services and community education services.

School Principal, Elizabeth Morris, is a psychologist, counsellor and trainer. She has also established the online Self-esteem Advisory Service in response to the increasing demand for information on this topic, as well as developing the Self Esteem Indicator as a diagnostic tool for assessing pupil's self-esteem. This is currently being published by NFER-Nelson. Elizabeth writes extensively on the subjects of self-esteem and emotional literacy, contributing a series of special reports for parents and a regular feature in *Primary Times*.

Elizabeth runs a Post Graduate Certificate in Emotional Literacy Development at Bristol University for any professional working with young people or families. The University of Bristol also runs her programmes on Emotional Intelligence and Self-motivation, Emotional Coaching and Self-esteem Building, all of which are open to parents as well as educators.

She is frequently interviewed on radio and in the press about emotional literacy development for children, and how to build self-esteem in families and classrooms.

Training and Inset Workshops

The School of Emotional Literacy offers a number of courses related to Self-Esteem, Emotional Literacy and brain-based learning and welcomes anyone interested in the development of children, pupils and young people to their training days and workshops.

Topics include:

- Introducing Emotional Literacy – Release the Potential in your School
- Puppets, Play and Poetry – great methods for developing self esteem and emotional literacy in pupils
- Emotional Coaching
- The Emotionally Literate Approach to Behaviour Management
- In what ways is that child intelligent?
- Using multiple intelligence theory in the classroom
- Building self-esteem in Children

For a full training list and for further information, please visit www.schoolofemotional-literacy.com, or call 01452 741106, or email info@schoolofemotional-literacy.com

Introduction

High self-esteem is one of the most important qualities a child can have. Research conducted in America by John Gottman at the University of Washington (1990 New York) has shown that children who have good self-esteem are better at relationships, better at understanding other people, better at managing their own emotions, better at calming themselves down, and more healthy! This is a pretty impressive list of benefits, and one that parents and teachers alike are keen to pass on to their children.

So how can you do this?

There are four main ways to help a child value themselves:

1. To love them
2. Value them
3. Treat them with respect
4. Give them many opportunities to build up their knowledge and skills, particularly in personal and social areas, these are the areas that boost self-esteem most when the child can manage them, but which drain it when they cannot.

Loving and valuing them

Having the knowledge that you are both loved and valued is very precious. Most children are aware that they are loved. They feel it when you look at them, when you care about when they are hurt or have concerns, when you take time to go over something they find hard, and acknowledge their triumphs with obvious pleasure. But feeling valued is more than that. It is about having respect from the adults in their lives and conveying that respect. In order to express this, adults must genuinely believe in the uniqueness of that child and acknowledge that they themselves have something to learn from the child, and not just that the child learns from them.

Being able to listen to the child's emotions, to follow their pace, to listen to their stories without judgement, and being able to talk so that the child has space to respond are all part of conveying respect and valuing children.

Valuing yourself

Children learn most efficiently by having someone to copy. Have you ever noticed how they do just what you do sometimes?

They'll sit with their hands under their chin; they'll use your tone of voice when they are talking to a friend, and they will pick up one of your habitual phrases and start using it as part of their everyday speech. You can use this fact about children's learning to help them develop good self-esteem.

For example, if they can see you dealing with difficult situations well and taking care of yourself because you believe you are important, they will begin to act like that too. If you feel good about yourself, you are more likely to enjoy the time you have with your class, rather than being distracted by having to complete reports, make up timetables or any of the other things that make up a working day. This way, a positive cycle can begin. It works this way:

You enjoy being with them because you feel good about yourself and are not spending time giving yourself a lot of negative messages. They enjoy their time with you because you're more fun and you make learning more enjoyable. They respond better to you and the subjects you are teaching. You enjoy that fact and feel even more positive about yourself, and so on.

This upwards spiral has spin-off benefits for both of you. It is easier to deal with difficulties in the classroom if the positive cycle has been working before.

Treating children with respect

As you give the children opportunities to think about themselves in relation to other people and to their own dreams, you are creating ideal conditions for the development of their self-esteem. These are conditions under which they can talk and reflect about themselves, and come to realise more and more about their abilities, strengths and impact. They can use their imagination to rehearse how to tackle difficult situations using the skills and strengths they already have. They can rehearse new skills and tactics too, and they can learn from each other if they have a chance to talk in a group about their work.

Giving them opportunities to build their personal and social skills

Using emotional coaching in the classroom situation helps children build their emotional literacy and is a very useful skill for you to learn. Emotional coaching is the process identified by John Gottman in the studies mentioned earlier. He identified five steps that parents took to help their children manage their emotional states constructively. These five steps helped children in wide variety of ways, from being physically healthier, to becoming more popular. The five steps can be done within a school or classroom context and we have found that this very useful to teach teachers. The five steps of emotional coaching are:

Step 1 Being aware of the pupil's emotions

Step 2 Recognising their emotion as an opportunity for relationship building and teaching

Step 3 Listening empathetically and validating the student's feelings

Step 4 Helping the student verbally label their emotions

Step 5 Helping the child solve the problem they are experiencing, including any imposed limits they may be struggling with

Doing projects together which help them learn more about themselves is another way to encourage their self-awareness. There are many of these projects in this resource and school sports or other play activities are all useful ways of giving children the opportunity to socialise and learn from one another.

A classroom format that has been proving very successful for helping children develop their social and personal abilities is Circle Time. This is a simple but structured technique of taking time in the classroom to sit in a circle, talking and listening to each other, discussing likes, dislikes, experiences and playing some co-operative games. It is particularly good for developing the self-awareness, social awareness, self-presentation and empathy of the students.

Emotional literacy

- "We have gone too far in emphasising the value and importance of the purely rational – what IQ measures. Intelligence comes to nothing when the emotions hold sway." (Daniel Goleman 1995)

- Emotional intelligence (or its practical application emotional literacy) have become very popular concepts in education. We ignore children's emotional self at our peril, for there is now an increasing weight of neurophysiological evidence that shows us how crucial the ability to make sense of our emotional states is to clear, creative and constructive thinking. The latest advances in brain science have shown us that we cannot make decisions without access to our emotions, and that uncontrolled emotion can seriously impair our ability to learn.

- *"Developing children as rounded people and active members of the community is at the heart of what schools are all about."* (Estelle Morris, Under Secretary of State for School Standards)

Developing emotional literacy in the classroom

Doing projects in the classroom together in pairs, small groups or as a whole class helps the children come to know themselves much better. It encourages self-reflection and also allows them to see how other children tackle the same issues. There is much they can learn from each other and you can help them make sense out of this by leading discussions about different ways of doing things and how many solutions there may be to problems. The children not only have an opportunity to learn more about themselves, they also have a chance to socialise and co-operate with one another. This forms another part of their social learning.

Making the activity a successful experience

It is crucial to the success of these activities that you praise the students while they are completing the tasks. If you do this by giving them specific feedback on what you like about what they have done, it will make your praise and direction far more meaningful and effective. They will be able to get even more information about their skills and strengths, as well as more subtle knowledge about the way they went about the project was acceptable. If they did it slowly that was OK. If they did a bit and then came back to it, that was OK too.

These are all ways that they learn to respect their own pace and creative style. This may not always fit into a busy school schedule, but within the parameters of the time you have set aside. The children can experience what it is like to do something their own way, and this is important personal learning.

Age ranges

The suggested age ranges in the next section are very flexible. Teachers should use their experience and discretion when deciding on sections or activities for their classes (for example, older but less able children will be able to work on the first three sections). Teachers should consider their pupils' maturity and confidence as well as their abilities. There may be a child with a specific problem – fear of storms for example – and this could influence the choice of the activities, but the teacher should be sensitive enough when handling the discussions not to allow the child to feel singled out and ashamed.

Social circumstances

Today, many children grow up in single parent homes, in blended families or in residential care. Similarly, there are many other children who are adopted, fostered or brought up by more distant blood relations. In building self-esteem activities it is particularly important that the teacher uses language that includes all possible situations and enables the pupils to feel comfortable, able and accepted in whatever their circumstances might be.

Wide range of abilities

Children in a classroom will exhibit a wide range of cognitive, physical, behavioural, social and emotional abilities. Many of these self-esteem building activities can be adapted to fit a wide range of abilities, and sensitivity will be needed when handling language and discussion.

How to use this resource

We suggest the following order of activities, as we have found they form a logical sequence for themes in the classroom:

1. All About Me, 5-7 years
2. Me and My World, 5-7 years
3. You and Me, 5-7 years
4. My Dreams and Wishes, 7-9 years
5. Daily Dilemmas, 9-11 years

Although we have arranged the resource in that order, the sections and the activities within any of them can also be easily used independently without having tackled previous sections. They are intended for class use and we have found them successful when used in the following ways:

a) The general format of the lesson would be to introduce the topic of each worksheet by discussion and then an explanation of the worksheet should follow.

b) The children can complete the sheets individually, in pairs or small groups. For some less able or less confident children, pairing or grouping might work better.

c) On completion of the sheets, another discussion would follow. Depending upon the topic the discussion could be in various forms, for example, during Circle Time, or a whole-class discussion, or in larger groups formed by joining two or three small groups, which are then 'led' by one of the students. This choice would be up to the teacher and is dependant on the sophistication of the class.

The sections were designed to be an aid in the teaching of a PSHE syllabus and so have been made as flexible as possible.

- A teacher could start each section at the beginning and work through it in order
- They can 'pick-and-mix' sheets to suit their class interests or yearly term themes
- They can select the activities that link to other areas of the curriculum

It is worth noting, however, that if a PSHE syllabus is being developed it is more beneficial to use the activities regularly than on an ad hoc basis.

All About Me

Teacher notes

The purpose of this section is to help the teacher learn more about the child and help the child learn more about themselves. They will find out:

- Their likes
- Their dislikes
- What makes them happy
- What makes them sad
- What their talents are

This should give an insight into the child and help the teacher understand them better, perhaps seeing new ways to help them learn, or understanding why they react the way they do in certain circumstances. This kind of knowledge can be invaluable when trying to manage difficult behaviour in the classroom. The section, once completed, may also help the child become more aware of their own feelings and behaviour. The children should also gain a sense of pride by sharing their special talents with others.

Some sheets require the child to write and, until they have this skill, an adult should write for the child. Therefore it may be easier, organisationally, for the teacher to give the sheet as a group lesson.

The worksheets in this section are all about things that will help the pupils think and learn about themselves and the environment they live in. We want to help them look again at what is around them and think about their relationship with these things. The section begins with 'Favourites' which are quite easy for pupils to recognise.

Worksheets 1 to 6 – My favourite things

The colour, food, at school, animals and TV programme sheets are for very young children and don't require much explanation. The teacher can pair two sheets together to make one lesson. The sheets can be extended by asking the child to write what their favourite colour reminds them of and why they chose it. Similar follow-up work can be done for the other favourite things sheet. Alternatively, the children can share their favourite things during Circle Time. For example "My favourite colour is… because…".

Worksheet 7 – Marvellous me

This worksheet enables children to be active, measuring themselves and each other in order to answer the questions. Another worksheet gives them prompts to think about other different qualities that are also 'marvellous' about them.

Worksheet 8 to 10 – My difference faces

These worksheets begin to explore emotions and develop the pupils' awareness of their body language. At a more subtle level, in **Worksheet 8 – My different faces** we are helping them notice that they can choose activities that can help them feel happier.
You may like to enlarge **Worksheet 10 – Mask** on the photocopier before handing this out.

Worksheet 11 – Music and me

Music can make us think of all kinds of things. In this activity play some music that is clearly 'happy', then play a piece that is slow and sad. Ask the pupils to say which was which. Then invite them to draw a picture of what the music reminded them of, or of how they felt when they listened to it. If they are finding that difficult, you can suggest that they might associate certain colours with feeling happy and other colours with feeling sad. Ask them what these colours might be.

Worksheet 12 – I am special sunshine

This worksheet is for helping children think again about their special qualities. In this exercise you can start suggesting things like a smile, their friendliness, their kindness, their creativity, their talents, and their interests. There are 8 qualities that they could fill in on the rays of the sun. If they struggle to fill that many in, you can ask them to move into small groups and help one another fill them in.

Worksheets 13 to 14 – I am special flag

These activities allow children to make a flag and use the information they developed on the sunshine worksheet. For example in the flags they can write one of the qualities that they are particularly proud of. They can also choose which flag they like best for themselves and colour that one in. The way that they all make them individual shows how unique everyone is.

Worksheet 15 to 16 – Who am I and Dear me

These worksheets use a pupil's writing and imaginative abilities. They are asked to write a poem about themselves and a letter to themselves. You could write a little poem to yourself to show them what to do "my name is Liz, I can get into a tiz, and run around, I sit down, my friends smile at me, I feel good and smile at them". You could do the same for the letter too.

Worksheet 17 – My name

This worksheet allows pupils to have fun with their names. It is a good one to do at the beginning of a new class or when a new pupil joins the group.

Worksheet 18 – My very best memory

Our memories are important sources of strength for us. For example, if we feel gloomy we can remember some enjoyable event. This activity helps the pupils build up a list of good memories to tap into whenever they like. You can refer back to this activity at other times – for instance, if it is a rainy day and the pupils are fed up you can suggest they go back to a sunny day memory. Talking about happy memories in Circle Time is an interesting topic too.

Worksheet 19 and 20 – How I feel and how I look

These worksheets help pupils learn more.

Circle Time suggestions to start a round

- My favourite colour is… because…
- My favourite food is…
- My favourite… etc
- I am happy/sad when…
- The music made me think of…
- The music reminded me of…
- The music made me feel…
- I am good at…
- I am special because…
- I can…
- I remember when…

Evaluation forms

These can be used to help the children learn how to assess their own experiences. The teacher can also assess the child's response to the lesson and template evaluation sheets follow.

All about me – pupil evaluation

Name .... Age .... Date ..../......./...........

Did I enjoy doing the sheet and having the discussion?

:) Yes, very much   :| It was OK   :(No, not at all

Worksheet

My favourite colour	
My favourite things to eat	
My favourite things at school	
My favourite things at home	
My favourite animal	
My favourite TV programme	
Marvellous me	
My different faces	
Mask	

Worksheet

Music and me	
I am special sunshine	
I am special flag	
Who am I?	
Dear me	
My name	
My very best memory	
How I feel and how I look inside	
How I feel and how I look outside	
The silliest songs in the world	

You will need: plain pencil, coloured pencil

All about me – teacher evaluation

Name .... Age .... Date ..../.........../...............

How did the child cope with the sheet and participate in the discussion?

S – Satisfactory   WH – With help from teacher/friends   D – Had some difficulty

Worksheet	S	WH	D
1. My favourite colour			
2. My favourite things to eat			
3. My favourite things at school			
4. My favourite things at home			
5. My favourite animal			
6. My favourite TV programme			
7. Marvellous me			
8. My different faces			
9. Mask			
10. Music and me			
11. I am special sunshine			
12. I am special flag			
13. Who am I?			
14. Dear me			
15. My name			
16. My very best memory			
17. How I feel and how I look inside			
18. How I feel and how I look outside			
19. The silliest songs in the world			

Favourite thing

Draw your favourite colour

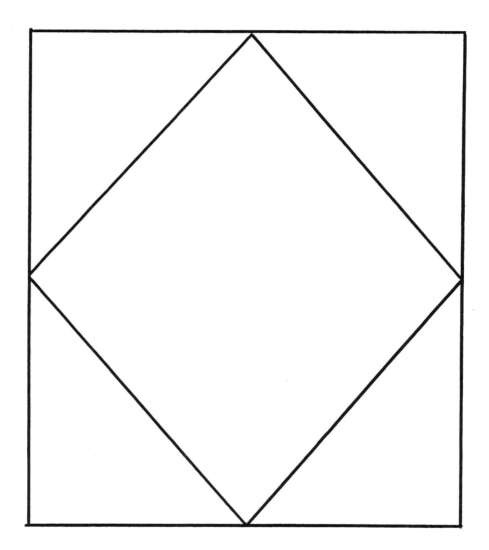

Name

. . . .

You will need: plain pencil, coloured pencils

Favourite thing

Draw your favourite things to eat

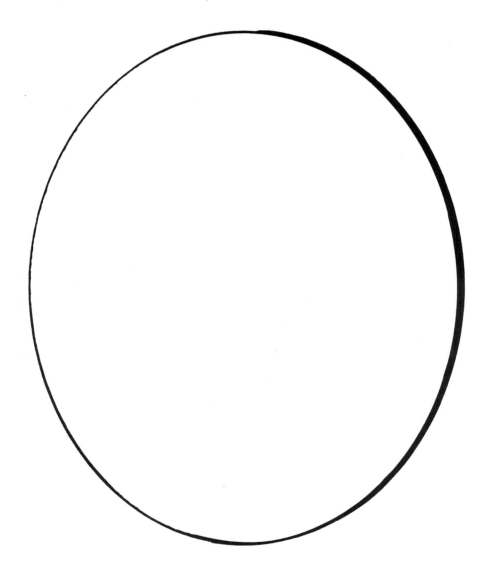

Name

. . . .

You will need: plain pencil, coloured pencils

All about me – Worksheet 2

Favourite thing

Draw your favourite things at school

Name

. . . .

You will need: plain pencil, coloured pencils

Favourite thing

Draw your favourite things at home

Name

. . . .

You will need: plain pencil, coloured pencils

All about me – Worksheet 4

Favourite thing

Draw your favourite animal

Name

. . . .

You will need: plain pencil, coloured pencils

Favourite thing

Draw your favourite TV programme

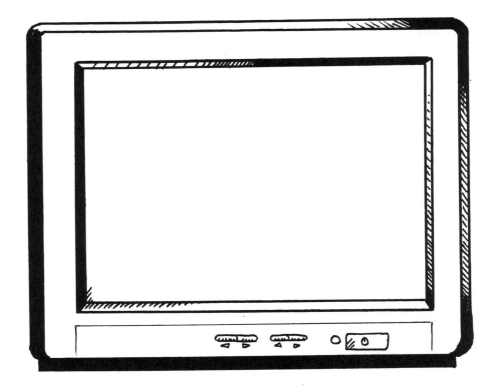

Name

....

You will need: plain pencil, coloured pencils

Marvellous me

I am [   ] tall

I have [   ] eyes

I have [   ] hair

I am wearing [   ]

My arms are [   ] long

My legs are [   ] long

Here I am – photograph or drawing

[   ]

Name

. . . .

You will need: plain pencil, coloured pencils

My different faces

When I feel happy I look like this:

Draw yourself here

Draw or write what makes you happy here

Name

....

You will need: plain pencil, coloured pencils

My different faces

When I feel sad I look like this:

Draw yourself here

Draw or write what makes you sad

_____

_____

_____

_____

_____

Name

. . . .

You will need: plain pencil, coloured pencils

Mask

Decorate and colour this mask. Make it happy, sad, afraid or angry.

Glue the face to some card, then leave it to dry. Cut along all the dotted lines then fold along the solid line. Use sticky tape to attach it to a lollipop stick or straw. Stick this to the back of the mask behind the chin.

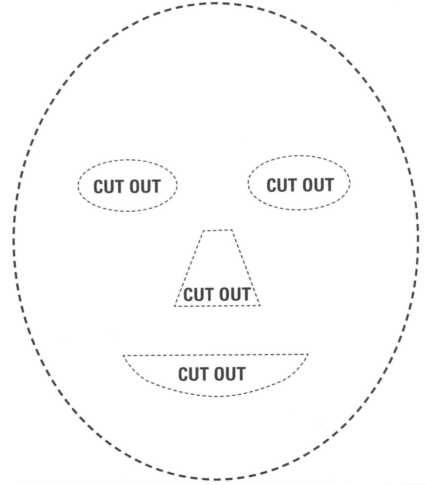

Name

. . . .

You will need: coloured pencils, card, glue, scissors, a stick and sticky tape

All about me – Worksheet 10

Music and me

Listen to some music. Decide if it sounded happy or sad. Paint a picture of what you heard.

Name

. . . .

You will need: plain pencil, coloured pencils or paints

I am special sunshine

What makes you special? Are you a good runner? Have you been somewhere special on holiday? Write down all the things that make you special on the rays of sunshine.

Name

. . . .

You will need: plain pencil, coloured pencils or paints

All about me – Worksheet 12

I am special flag

Choose a flag you like. Colour it in and cut it out. Use some sticky tape to stick one side of it to a straw.

HURRAH! Wave your flag because you are special.

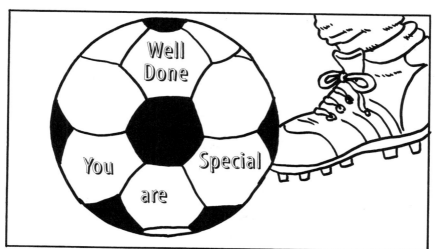

Name

. . . .

You will need: coloured pencils, scissors, a straw and sticky tape

I am special flag

Choose a flag you like. Colour it in and cut it out. Use some sticky tape to stick one side of it to a straw.

HURRAH! Wave your flag because you are special.

Name

. . . .

You will need: coloured pencils, scissors, a straw and sticky tape

Who am I?

Draw a picture of yourself here or paste in a photograph

Now write a poem called 'I Am...' It doesn't have to rhyme.

_____

_____

_____

_____

_____

Name

. . . .

You will need: plain pencil, coloured pencils, photograph (optional) scissors, a straw and sticky tape and glue

Dear me...

Write a letter to yourself. In this letter tell yourself all the things you really like about yourself as if you were writing to another person.

When you're feeling sad you can read this letter to yourself and you will feel much better.

Name

. . . .

You will need: plain pencil

My name

Make a design using each letter of your name. This is your special logo.

Name

. . . .

You will need: plain pencil, coloured pencils

My very best memory

Try to remember something that you really liked – a day, a birthday, Christmas – write the story and then draw a picture of it.

My story

_____

_____

_____

_____

_____

_____

Name

. . . .

You will need: plain pencil, coloured pencils

How I feel and how I look inside

On this page draw how you feel inside.

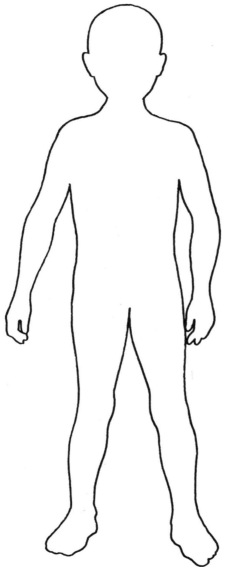

Name

. . . .

You will need: plain pencil, coloured pencils

How I feel and how I look outside

On this page draw how you look on the outside.

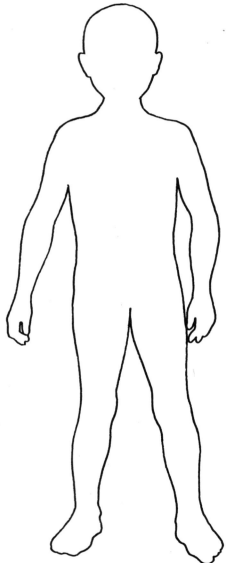

Name

....

You will need: plain pencil, coloured pencils

All about me – Worksheet 20

The silliest songs in the world

Write a silly song all about yourself. Use words that sound the same or words that sound funny.

_____

_____

_____

_____

_____

_____

_____

_____

_____

_____

Name

. . . .

You will need: plain pencil, music

Me and My World

Teacher notes

In this section we are helping pupils to begin to consider themselves in relation to their world. This includes the place they live in, their school, the town, buildings, the natural world, weather and seasons. The aim of the section is to start children thinking about themselves as part of a society, not just in relation to themselves and their own feelings or their close relationships, but looking much wider, taking in the cultures they live in and the natural environment. As always in these sections, the pupils are encouraged to think about themselves and their own feelings and responses to the wider world. The reason for this is that the more comfortable and adept the children are in considering and demonstrating their feeling responses, the more emotionally literate they will be as they grow up. As neurophysiology and brain research is showing, the learning processes that children experience actually help their frontal lobes (part of the neo-cortex in the brain) mature and make connections with the emotional processing capacity of the limbic system. In turn, this increasingly enables them to problem solve, self soothe and have good coping strategies in the face of complex stressors. These developing emotional competencies all help a child have good self-esteem and an effective 'can-do' attitude.

Worksheet 1 – Myself

This worksheet starts the section by focusing firstly on the child before moving out into the wider world. This worksheet sets the scene and can be done quite quickly before starting the next worksheet. Suggest to the child that they draw themselves, but do not colour it in so that they can concentrate on the details of the picture.

Worksheet 2 – Me and my home

Now the pupils focus on their home and begin to notice what kind of house it is compared to others. These exercises help children observe. We often fail to notice what is under our own noses because we are so familiar with it. As the children complete the worksheets, you can ask them to discuss how long they have been in their home, how many people live there, whether there is a garden or small plant boxes, if birds visit their homes and how they would feel about moving from their home and finding another one at some time.

Suggestion

- Older children can develop this worksheet by including a plan of their bedroom on the back of the sheet
- In Circle Time a round could be started with "I live…"

Worksheet 3 – School

Next the pupils will consider their school, what it looks like and how it might be different from a school they have been at previously. They need to observe or recall carefully and then draw it in detail. If the school is large they can decide which part they might want to draw. Different children can draw different areas so that, in total, the class will produce a set of drawings of the whole school. As in the previous exercise, the children can discuss an aspect of their school as they work through the sheet. They can discuss what they like most about the buildings, what they like least, how they felt when they first arrived, and how they feel now. Do they feel like they belong to the school or are they still feeling uncertain?

Worksheet 4 – Shops

This worksheet takes the child and their powers of observation into the town, village or city and encourages them to observe the different types of shops they might see. They can choose which ones they would like to draw. If there is a market in the town, they can draw parts of that. Different children can draw different shops and parts of a high street, for example. As the children work through the worksheet they can discuss which shops they visit and why, what they buy in these shops, who they go with, how often they go and which shops they like and why. These exercises all help children make connections with their world and observe not only the detail surrounding them but also their own responses, likes and preferences to them.

Worksheet 5 – Me and my street

In this worksheet the children focus on their neighbourhood. They will observe and remember houses, shops and people who are located near their own home. They can choose which part of this area to draw and their choices are all acceptable. Try not to judge and criticise what they decide to draw, but ask them what the aspect they have chosen means to them. The class discussion can include the names of people who live near them, whether they have visited any of the other places, and whether they looked similar to their own home.

Worksheet 6 – Me and my town

In this worksheet the pupil will look again at the town or nearest town to where they live. This time they will look at the public buildings, rather than the shops. They can choose their favourite building and draw that. In this choice they can discuss whether they are drawing the building that they enjoy most because they like the shape, size or colour of the building, or because they like the activity that it houses. Either choice is fine and should be encouraged. The discussion in the class can be around the ways that town councils provide the people with public buildings and services and what they would like to see in their town.

Suggestion

- In Circle Time the round could start with "My favourite building in my town is… because…"
- An additional activity could be to cut out the buildings that pupils have drawn and to place them all on a large piece of paper to make a representation of the town. The children will decide how to place the buildings on the paper and this would be the start of a map of the area. Don't worry about scale, or that it won't be a view from above – that is a hard concept to manage. If you are mapping a large town, just break it down and decide which part you will focus on.

Worksheet 7 – Getting to school

This worksheet helps pupils connect with the outer world through becoming aware of the ways they can travel. The worksheet is essentially about travelling to school, but discussion in the class can branch out to talk about journeys to and from other places. What form of transport do the children like or not like? What was the longest journey they have ever made?

Suggestion

■ You can collect information on the various methods of transport that the pupils use and create a class graph to show what the most common and least common method is in the class.

Worksheet 8 – Winter feelings

In this worksheet children are asked to notice themselves and their feelings when it is wintertime. Some people love it – they like the cold and crisp weather, they like the feeling that it's nearly Christmas. Perhaps their birthday is in that season. These are all aspects that can be developed in a class discussion. An aim in the exercise is to help children notice that they have reactions to the external world, that something as subtle and quietly pervasive as a season can influence how a person feels. It also prompts a child to think about their friendships too, and to imagine them all building a snowman.

Worksheet 9 – Winter cold

In this worksheet more observation and memory is necessary (if doing this activity in another season). Pupils are asked to take note of how they will respond to the season by choosing different clothes to suit the activities that fit the time of year. They will be thinking of the things they do then that differ from the activities they do at other times. This can lead into class discussion about the people they do activities with, to what people do in countries where it is wintry for much of the year. They can be asked to think about living in a country where it is hot and summery for much of the year, or where it never snows. How would they feel in an environment like that? With younger children, give them some help to make sure that they choose activities that are relevant to this time of year.

Worksheet 10 – Winter events

In this worksheet they will be writing about the things they do at this time of year. Typically the commercial world encourages everyone to celebrate Christmas, but this is different for people from other cultures and religions. In the class, volunteers can talk about what they have written and the class can discuss how the activities are similar and different. The activities that they write about can be as diverse as going for winter walks or to new year parties.

Worksheet 11 – Summer feelings

In this worksheet children are asked to notice themselves and their feelings when it is summertime. Some people like the warmth, the soft fruit, that holidays are near and maybe their birthday is in that season. These are all aspects that can be developed in a class discussion. An aim in the exercise is to help children notice that they have reactions to the external world, that something as subtle and quietly pervasive as a season can influence how a person feels. It also prompts a child to think about their likes and dislikes and what they might look forward to as the season approaches.

Worksheet 12 – Summer events

In this worksheet more observation and memory is necessary (if doing this activity in another season). Pupils are asked to take note of how they will respond to the season by choosing different clothes to suit the activities that fit the time of year. They will be thinking of the things they do then that differ from the activities they do at other times.

This can lead into class discussion about the people they do activities with, to what people do in countries where it is hot and summery for much of the year or where it never rains. How would they feel in an environment like that? With younger children give them some help to make sure they choose activities that are relevant to this time of year.

Worksheet 13 – Summertime

In this worksheet they will be writing about the things they do at this time of year. Typically it is holiday time so they may spend more time with important people, their friends or they may go away for a while and have different experiences in other countries or parts of Britain. Each person will have a different experience of summer that they can do some creative writing about. In the class, volunteers can talk about what they have written and the class can discuss how the activities are similar and different. The activities that they write about can be as diverse as going to the beach to having cool drinks rather than warm ones.

Worksheet 14 – Autumn feelings

In this worksheet children are asked to notice themselves and their feelings when it is autumn. Some people like the colours, the slowing down, the different temperature and maybe their birthday is in that season. These are all aspects that can be developed in a class discussion. An aim in the exercise is to help children notice that they have reactions to the external world, that something as subtle and quietly pervasive as a season can influence how a person feels. It also prompts a child to think about their likes and dislikes and what they might look forward to as the season approaches.

Worksheet 15 – Things I do in autumn

In this worksheet more observation and memory is necessary (if doing this activity in another season). Pupils are asked to take note of how they will respond to the season by choosing different clothes to suit the activities that fit the time of year. They will be thinking of the things they do then that differ from the activities they do at other times. This can lead into class discussion about the people they do activities with, to what people do in countries where there is no autumn season. Or discussions about countries such as America or Canada where the trees turn spectacular shades of red and gold. What happens in other countries? How would they feel in an environment like that? With younger children give them some help to make sure that they choose activities that are relevant to this time of year.

Worksheet 16 – Autumn events

In this worksheet the children will be writing about the things they do at this time of year. Typically it is wet and windy and festivals such as Halloween occur. Pupils from different cultures and religions will have different events that they will enjoy and be engaged in during this time. Each person will have a different experience of autumn that they can do some creative writing about. In the class, volunteers can talk about what they have written and the class can discuss how the activities are similar and different. The activities that they write about can be as diverse as splashing through puddles to playing with conkers.

Worksheet 17 – Spring feelings

In this worksheet children are asked to notice themselves and their feelings when it is springtime. Some people like the new growth appearing in gardens, the slight change of temperature and the birdsong. Maybe their birthday is in that season. These are all aspects that can be developed in a class discussion. An aim in the exercise is to help children notice that they have reactions to the external world, that something as subtle and quietly pervasive as a season can influence how a person feels. It also prompts a child to think about their likes and dislikes and what they might look forward to as the season approaches.

Worksheet 18 – Spring flower favourites

In this worksheet some common spring flowers are drawn and it calls upon observation and memory from the pupils again. This is an opportunity to notice the children in the class who may have a strong 'naturalist intelligence'. This is one of the eight multiple intelligences identified by Howard Gardner and means that the child is highly attuned to the natural world and aware of the relationships between and within ecosystems. These children have probably been quite interested in the preceding worksheets as they have been exploring a natural phenomenon such as the weather and seasons.

Suggestion

- The children may need some help with naming and spelling the flower names. They tend to be more familiar with the daffodil and tulip and some help will be required with the snowdrop and crocus.
- The exercise can lead to discussions of different flowers, which flowers or trees are going to bloom in that season and what other flowers bloom in the other seasons.

As usual with this resource, it is always a good idea to ask the children what they like about flowers, what they dislike, how they feel when they see the first signs of new plants appearing, and what they have noticed that other people feel.

Worksheet 19 – Spring things to do

In this worksheet more observation and memory is necessary (if doing this activity in another season). Pupils are asked to take note of how they will respond to the season by choosing different clothes to suit the activities that fit the time of year. They will be thinking of the things they do then that differ from the activities they do at other times. This can lead into class discussion about the people they do activities with, to what people do in countries where there is little or no spring season. How would they feel in an environment like that? With younger children give them some help to make sure that they chose activities that are relevant to this time of year.

Worksheet 20 – Spring events

In this worksheet they will be writing about the things they do at this time of year. Typically it is windy and beginning to get warmer. Festivals such as Easter occur. Pupils from different cultures and religions will have different events that they will enjoy and be engaged in during this time. Each person will have a different experience of spring that they can do some creative writing about. In the class, volunteers can talk about what they have written and the class can discuss how the activities are similar and different. The activities that they write about can be as diverse as watching lambs jump and play, to a half-term treat.

Worksheet 21 – Seasons

In these worksheets we are asking the pupils to think about the trees in their world and how they look at different times of the year. A discussion can then take place on how they like each season's trees. What are the advantages of trees being covered in leaves. What are the advantages of bare trees? What is the tree doing while it is bare?

Worksheet 22 – My favourite season

The worksheet helps to pull together all the thinking and awareness that they have been developing over the preceding activities. It starts to focus again on the pupil and their response, feelings and preferences. It helps them re-affirm some good memories so that they can help themselves feel better at times when they feel a bit blue. This is part of a self-esteem and emotional literacy development programme. They are learning ways to regulate their emotions as they make discoveries through doing the worksheets and taking part in the discussions.

Worksheet 23 to 25 – The class thunderstorm: clouds, lightning and raindrops

These worksheets give the pupils an opportunity to build a mobile while they become aware of the feelings they have when there is a thunderstorm. An option is to make a class display on the wall when pupils have written their feelings on the images of different aspects of a storm. This exercise helps them think about the natural world and how it impacts on them. The class can discuss and explore ways to deal with these feelings as part of an emotional literacy development process. Remember that emotional literacy helps self-esteem enormously.

Suggestion

- In Circle Time a round can start with:

  "During a thunderstorm I feel…

  I feel better when I…"

Worksheet 26 – Special time

This worksheet helps pupils remember good times and so reinforces their memories of the feelings and sensations they had during that event. This building up of a 'portfolio' of happy memories is great as a resource for children to turn to if they are having a hard time at some point. The self soothing activity helps them to feel more in charge of their reactions and helps them be more resiliant when there are many stressors affecting them. Giving the children this kind of information and reminding them that they can use their memories in this way slowly teaches them new strategies for handling their emotions.

Me and my world – pupil evaluation

Name .... Age .... Date ..../......./..........

Did I enjoy doing the sheet and having the discussion?

 Yes, very much  It was OK No, not at all

Worksheet		Worksheet	
Myself		Things I do in autumn	
Me and my home		Autumn events	
School		Spring feelings	
Shops		Spring things to do	
Me and my street		Spring events	
Me and my town		Seasons	
Getting to school		My favourite season	
Winter feelings		The class thunderstorm – clouds	
Winter cold			
Winter events		The class thunderstorm – lightning	
Summer feelings			
Summer events		The class thunderstorm – raindrops	
Summer time			
Autumn feelings		Special time	

You will need: plain pencil, coloured pencils

Me and my world – teacher evaluation

Name .... Age .... Date ..../......./..........

How did the child cope with the sheet and participate in the discussion?

S – Satisfactory   WH – With help from teacher/friends   D – Had some difficulty

Worksheet	S	WH	D
1. Myself			
2. Me and my home			
3. School			
4. Shops			
5. Me and my street			
6. Me and my town			
7. Getting to school			
8. Winter feelings			
9. Winter cold			
10. Winter events			
11. Summer feelings			
12. Summer events			
13. Summer time			
14. Autumn feelings			
15. Things I do in autumn			
16. Autumn events			
17. Spring feelings			
18. Spring flower favourites			
19. Spring things to do			
20. Spring events			
21. Seasons			
22. My favourite season			
23. The class thunderstorm – clouds			
24. The class thunderstorm – lightning			
25. The class thunderstorm – raindrops			
26. Special time			

Myself

Draw yourself

This is me

My full name is

_____

Name

. . . .

You will need: plain pencil, coloured pencils

Me and My World – Worksheet 1

Me and my home

Draw a picture of where you live. Think about where you will put yourself in the picture. Now add yourself to the picture.

This is me and my house.

Name

. . . .

You will need: plain pencil, coloured pencils

School

Draw a picture of your school.

My school is called

_____

Name

. . . .

You will need: plain pencil, coloured pencils

Shops

Draw some of the shops in your town.

SUPERMARKET

NEWSAGENT

Write down the names of some of the shops in your town.

_____

_____

_____

_____

Name

. . . .

You will need: plain pencil, coloured pencils

Me and my street

Draw some of the buildings in your town. Remember they won't all look exactly the same.

Here is my street.

My address is

_____

_____

_____

Name
. . . .
You will need: plain pencil, coloured pencils

Getting to school

How do you get to school?

Draw a picture of yourself going to school.

Who is with you?

Write down their names

_____

_____

_____

Name

. . . .

You will need: plain pencil, coloured pencils

Me and my town

Does your town have special buildings like a library, a swimming pool or a railway station? Draw some of your favourite buildings.

STATION

SCHOOL

I live in

Name

. . . .

You will need: plain pencil, coloured pencils

Winter feelings

How do you feel when it's winter?

Write some words to describe how you feel inside the snow flake.

In winter I feel:

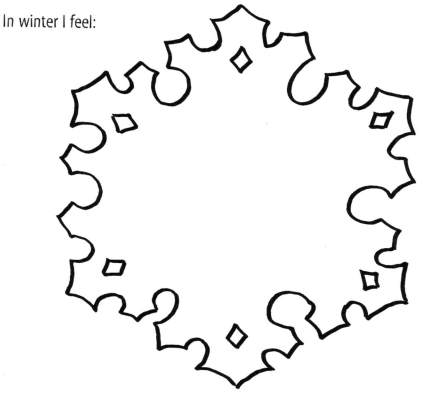

Which friends would help you build a snowman?

_____

_____

Name

. . . .

You will need: plain pencil

Winter cold

Paint a picture of special things you can do only in the winter.
Think about the weather and the clothes you wear.

Name

. . . .

You will need: plain pencil, some paints, a brush

Winter events

Write about the special things that happen in winter.

_____

_____

_____

_____

_____

_____

_____

_____

_____

Name

. . . .

You will need: plain pencil

Summer feelings

How do you feel when it's summer?

Write some words to describe how you feel inside the ice cream cone and lollies. Remember you can add more if you want to.

In summer I feel:

What kind of ice cream or lolly do you like best?

_____

Name

. . . .

You will need: plain pencil

Summer events

Paint a picture of some things you can do in summer. Think of the clothes you wear and remember that the weather is warmer.

Name

. . . .

You will need: plain pencil, paints, a brush

Summertime

Write about what special things happen in summer.

_____

_____

_____

_____

_____

_____

_____

_____

_____

_____

Name

. . . .

You will need: plain pencil

Autumn feelings

How do you feel when it's autumn? Write some words to describe how
you feel inside the kite and leaf.

In autumn I feel:

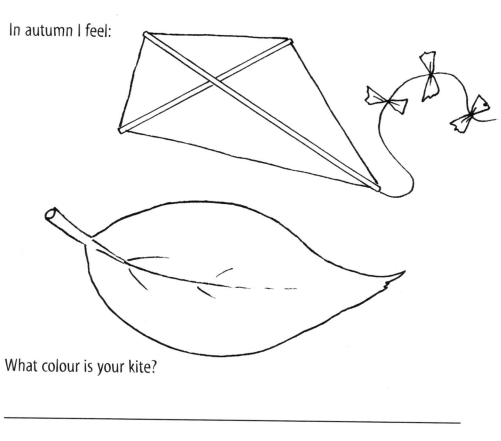

What colour is your kite?

_____

What colours do the leaves turn in autumn?

_____

Name

. . . .

You will need: plain pencil

Things I do in autumn

Paint a picture of the things you can only do in autumn. Remember it is probably wet and windy.

Name

. . . .

You will need: plain pencil, some paints, a brush

Autumn events

Write down the special things that happen in autumn

_____

_____

_____

_____

_____

_____

_____

_____

_____

_____

Name

. . . .

You will need: plain pencil

Spring feelings

How do you feel when it's spring? Write some words to describe how you feel inside the flower.

In spring I feel:

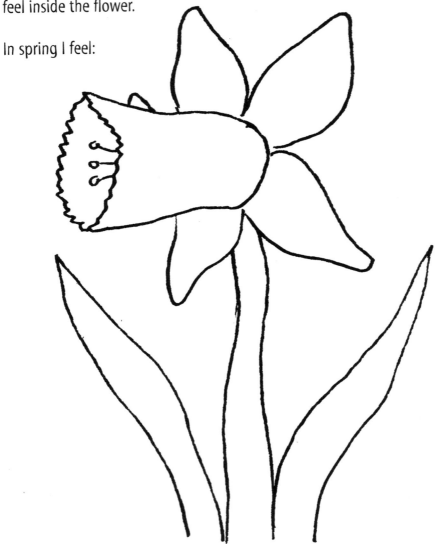

Name

. . . .

You will need: plain pencil

Me and My World – Worksheet 17

Spring flower favourites

Write the name of each flower on the lines below, then colour the flower in.

_____

_____

_____

_____

_____

_____

_____

_____

_____

_____

_____

_____

Name

. . . .

You will need: plain pencil, coloured pencils

Spring things to do

Paint a picture of the things you do in spring. Think what the weather is like in spring.

Name

. . . .

You will need: plain pencil, some paint, a brush

Spring events

Write about some special things that happen in spring.

_____

_____

_____

_____

_____

_____

_____

_____

_____

_____

_____

Name

. . . .

You will need: plain pencil

Seasons

What would you add to each scene to show the changes in the season?

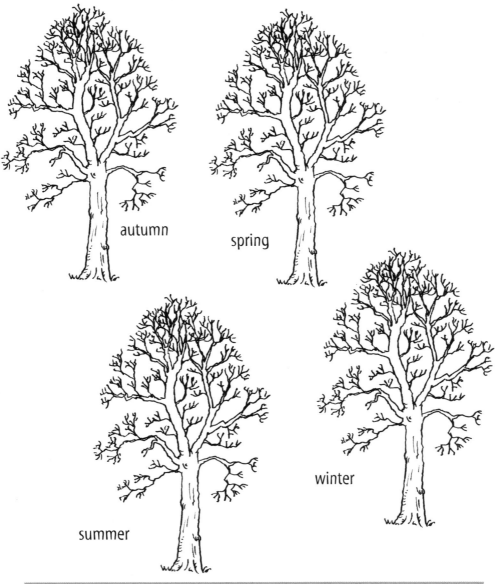

autumn

spring

summer

winter

Name

. . . .

You will need: plain pencil, some paint, a brush

Me and My World – Worksheet 21

My favourite season

My favourite season is:

_____

_____

_____

_____

_____

I like this time of year best because:

_____

_____

_____

_____

_____

_____

_____

Name
. . . .
You will need: plain pencil

The class thunderstorm

Write some words inside the clouds to show how you feel during a thunderstorm.

Cut out the clouds and stick them onto some card. Leave them to dry. Cut the card around the shapes and stick some lengths of wool between the shapes to make a mobile.

Name

. . . .

You will need: plain pencil, glue, card, scissors, wool

Me and My World – Worksheet 23

The class thunderstorm

Write some words inside the strikes of lightning to show how you feel during a thunderstorm.

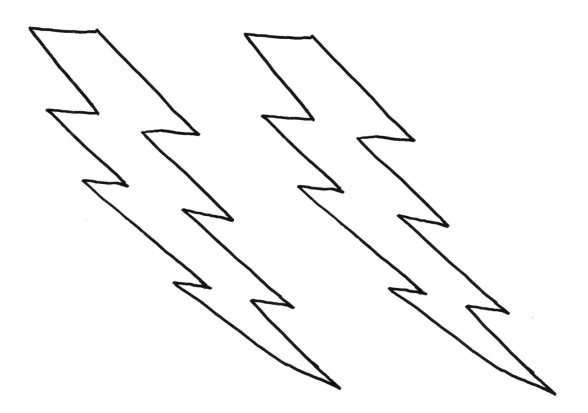

Cut out the strikes of lightning and stick them onto some card. Leave them to dry. Cut the card around the shapes and stick some lengths of wool between the shapes to make a mobile. Add the lightning strikes below the clouds.

Name

. . . .

You will need: plain pencil, glue, scissors, card, wool

The class thunderstorm

Write some words inside the raindrops to show how you feel during a thunderstorm.

Cut out the raindrops and stick them onto some card. Leave them to dry. Cut the card around the shapes and stick some lengths of wool between the shapes to make a mobile. Add your raindrops below the clouds and around the lightning strikes to complete the mobile.

Name

. . . .

You will need: plain pencil, glue, scissors, card, wool

Special time

Try to remember a really special time you've had. It could be a friend's birthday, Christmas or a great summer holiday.

Draw a picture of your special time. Use different materials, cut into small pieces and glue them onto your picture to make a collage.

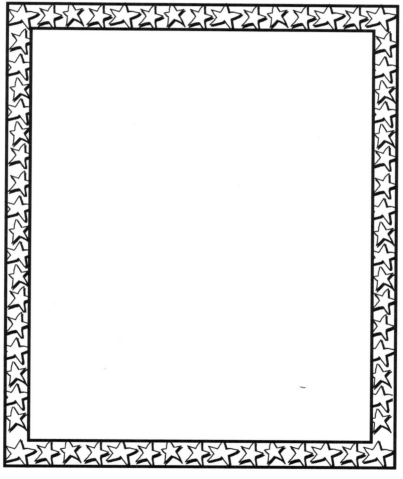

Name

. . . .

You will need: plain pencil, glue, scissors, various textures, plain and patterned

You and Me

Teacher notes

This section focuses on the child and their social relationships with a variety of important people. The purpose of the section is to help the child realise what connections they have with other people and how important these connections are. It will help them define the wider context of their family and peer group. The section also aims to help them communicate better within these contexts.

Worksheet 1 – My important people portrait

This worksheet starts pupils thinking about the important people in their lives. Who will they choose to put in the portrait? They might want to include pets. The lesson can be preceded by a discussion about relationships and how we have connections with all kinds of people, from the ones we live with, to friends, neighbours, or people we have met once or twice but who left an impression on us. It is the child's choice. Along with their own portrait, they can draw in as many other important people as they like.

Suggestion

- Follow-up activities – create a display including their drawn portraits and encourage children to bring in photographs of their important people. Cut out similar pictures from magazines and include these in the display too.

- You can compare the different numbers of important people in the different portraits. Remember not to imply that any particular number is better than another. However many important people the child has is fine. The different numbers can be represented in a graph.

- Discuss important people. What makes them important? Is it their personal qualities? Their family connection? Their actions?

Worksheet 2 and 3 – Me and my important people tree

This worksheet is a follow on or alternative to the previous worksheet on the portrait. It helps pupils see the variety of people they think of as important to them. Again it can be introduced in a discussion about relationships and people we are connected with because they are important to us. These discussions help children reaffirm their sense of belonging which is an important component of self-esteem.

Suggestion

- Alternatives can be to make a tree using the names of pupils in the class or the school. This will help pupils form a more cohesive group with an idea of them all being connected with one another in a particular way

- Discuss the positioning of the specific leaves. Where did the child place themselves? Where did the child place their parent/carers? Why were they placed there?

- For Me and My School you can make leaves and ask everyone in the school to write their name on them on one side and draw a self-portrait on the other. Include all staff. Where does the headteacher go in comparison to the class teacher? What about the janitor, cleaners and cooks?

Worksheet 4 – Happy times

If time is short then a drawing would be sufficient to illustrate the happy time. Also magazines, newspapers and so on can also be used in the collage.

Suggestion

- Additional activites – the notes on the back of the picture can be discussed and developed into a story. An adult may have to scribe for a younger child or they can be taped on video or audio.
- In Circle Time a round can be started with "My family had a happy time when…"

Worksheet 5 – Important people song

This worksheet carries on the theme of important people. You can refer to a previous session you have had on this and say that this time you are going to celebrate all these important people in a different way – by making up a song.

Keep the song short and snappy. It could be in the form of a rap or cheerleader chant. Children should be allowed to help each other out. If they are stuck, give them a start:

"We're the best because we're OK"

"We have fun all of the day…"

Suggestion

- To add some extra movements to the exercise you can include some simple moves like clapping, knee slapping and finger snapping. Each group of children could demonstrate one of the songs or a few children could volunteer their songs and the rest of the class can provide the background sounds such as clapping in rhythm.

Worksheet 6 – Letterbox

This worksheet can be used most successfully in a one to one session or in a small tutorial group. It is quite sensitive to manage in a large class and we would suggest that you only use it in the more personal contact of a one-to-one or smaller groups. Some sensitive discussion may be needed if a pupil gets very upset after an event and then reconnects with that when they remember it. Rather than only dwelling on the negative feelings, the discussion or session could be used to help children realise what a variety of ways there are to deal with their emotions for example, listen to music, take a walk, talk to someone, writing it out in a letter etc.

Worksheet 7 – Friendship web

The teacher can introduce the lesson on the blackboard telling pupils that the lesson is going to be about friendships and that they are going to learn how to draw their own friendship web. Choose a popular uninhibited child (A) and write their name in the middle of the board. Draw a circle round their name. Ask (A) who is your best friend? They reply (B) so you have:

Ask B, do you like A? – Yes so you have:

Then continue asking A about some friends until you have a spider web effect. The children can then go and start their own sheets. Remind the children to keep the diagram large so it doesn't become cluttered. If it happens that B says No! (which doesn't usually happen) you can affirm that it is OK to have A likes B and for B not necessarily to like A. You can then ask B who they like.

An additional activity would be to include relationships between friends. Do B and C get on?

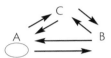

Worksheet 8 – My best friend

If a child says they don't have a best friend then they can certainly write down what sort of person they would like to be their best friend. What would they do together?

Worksheet 9 – My friends and I

This worksheet identifies what things children do with their friends, and the task of making a paper chain highlights how friends link together.

Worksheet 10 – Same or different

This worksheet also helps pupils focus on their special friends and begin to articulate and understand what it is that draws them to certain people. You can start the lesson by taking two children as examples. Discuss hair colour, eye colour, size, clothes and so on.

Suggestion

- In Circle Time a round can start with: " My friend and I have the same… " or
  "I admire my friend's…"

Worksheet 11 – Mirror dance

In this worksheet friends or 'neighbours' can work with one another in pairs. They have to learn how to mirror one another and so learn how to attend and observe very carefully. You can show some movements with a child as a demonstration, pointing out that if you move your right arm, then they must move the left. A lot of practice is necessary to enable the children to remember a sequence of moves. Keep it simple so that they can achieve a short dance together successfully.

Worksheet 12 – Making up with my friends

Learning how to manage friendships and relationships is an important part of a child's education since they will spend the rest of their lives having to make, break and maintain relationships with others. These two worksheets look at how you feel when you fall out with friends, and how you feel and what you do to make up with them. You can start by discussing a time you fell out with a friend and then ask for volunteers who can tell you about a time they fell out with a friend. Help them describe how they felt and how they made up with their friend. After this demonstration the class can then complete their own worksheets. Following that you can begin a discussion to draw their attention to the different ways people make up, and perhaps how some people don't make up. Again, make no judgements about this so that the children feel free to talk about what happened. Some children will laugh about it now, but will also remember that at the time they felt differently. Discuss how they made up. Why did they fall out?

Worksheet 14 – Friendship poem

The important aspects of this worksheet is that the children work with a friend. Try to ensure this is a co-operative venture and that it is lots of fun.

Worksheet 15 – Hearts

This worksheet encourages pupils to tell or show people who are important to them how they feel. They can give the 'hearts' to their friends, family or important people. They can talk with each other or in the class discussion about how they would feel if someone gave them a heart. Sometimes the children may want to change the wording. Suggestions would be: I like you because…I care about you because…I am fond of you because…

Worksheet 16 and 17 – Special person awards

Explain to the children that the special person can be absolutely anyone – friends or family. You could have a special person presentation. Preparation is essential to ensure that everyone receives something, even if the teacher has to make some medals or certificates herself. Nobody should feel left out. Invitations could be made to ask recipients to attend. Provide refreshments. and decorate the classroom.

You and me – pupil evaluation

Name .... Age .... Date ..../......./...........

Did I enjoy doing the sheet and having the discussion?

:) Yes, very much   :| It was OK   :(No, not at all

Worksheet

My important people portrait	
Me and my important people tree 1	
Me and my important people tree 2	
Happy Times	
Important people song	
Letterbox	
Friendship web	
My best friend	
My friends and I	

Worksheet

Same or different	
Mirror dance	
Making up with my friends 1	
Making up with my friends 2	
Friendship poem	
Hearts	
Special person award 1	
Special person award 2	

You will need: plain pencil, coloured pencil

You and me – teacher evaluation

Name .... Age .... Date ..../.........../.............

How did the child cope with the sheet and participate in the discussion?

S – Satisfactory   WH – With help from teacher/friends   D – Had some difficulty

Worksheet	S	WH	D
1. My important people portrait			
2. Me and my important people tree 1			
3. Me and my important people tree 2			
4. Happy times			
5. Important people song			
6. Letterbox			
7. Friendship web			
8. My best friend			
9. My friends and I			
10. Same or different?			
11. Mirror dance			
12. Making up with my friends 1			
13. Making up with my friends 2			
14. Friendship poem			
15. Hearts			
16. Special person award 1			
17. Special person award 2			

My important people portrait

Draw a picture of yourself. Then draw your 'important people' behind and around you. You can draw friends, neighbours, your pets, brothers, sisters, grandmother, teacher, grandfathers, aunts, foster parents, whoever and whatever matters to you.

This is me and my important people.

This is a list of my important people:

me...

...

...

...

Name
. . . .
You will need: plain pencil, coloured pencils

You and Me – Worksheet 1

Me and my important people tree 1

In each leaf write the name of one person or being who is important to you. Don't forget yourself. Cut them out and stick them onto the tree on the next sheet.

Think carefully about where you put each person. Where will you put yourself? Where will you put each person, are some connected with each other as well as you? Colour the tree and the leaves.

If there aren't enough leaves draw more of your own.

Name

. . . .

You will need: plain pencil, scissors, glue

Me and my important people tree 2

My family tree by:

_____

Name

. . . .

You will need: plain pencil, coloured pencils

Happy times

Shut your eyes and remember one happy time with one or more of your important people. Draw a picture of this time. Cut out some different coloured and patterned material and stick it onto your picture to make it into a collage. Write down below what made this time so happy.

Name

. . . .

You will need: plain pencil, scissors, glue, a variety of fabric

Important people song

Make up a song, poem, rap or chant about you and your important people. It doesn't have to rhyme.

Name

. . . .

You will need: plain pencil

You and Me – Worksheet 5

Letterbox

Write a letter to someone whose actions have upset you in the past.
Perhaps they have argued with you, or with someone else and you ended
up feeling unhappy or scared or annoyed. The letter will explain how you
have felt at these times. Draw pictures instead of words if you prefer.

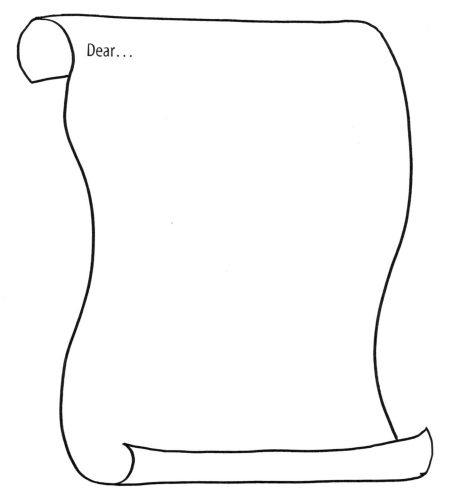

Dear...

Name

. . . .

You will need: plain pencil, coloured pencils

Friendship web

Write your name in the middle of the circle and your friends names around the outside. Draw a line between yourself and every one of your friends to make a sort of web.

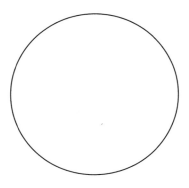

Name
....
You will need: plain pencil, coloured pencils

My best friend

Do you have a best friend?

If you do, draw him or her here. You can draw more than one friend
if you like.

My best friend is

_____

What makes this friend so special?

_____

_____

_____

Name

. . . .

You will need: plain pencil, coloured pencils

My friends and I

What sort of things do you do with your friends? Write in the boxes and cut them out. Glue the ends together and join them by linking them into a paper chain. Keep the writing on the outside.

My friends and I

My friends and I

My friends and I

My friends and I

My friends and I

My friends and I

Name

. . . .

You will need: plain pencil, scissors, glue

Same or different?

Draw yourself here

Draw your friend here

Which parts look the same? Join them up with a line.

What do you admire about your friend?

_____

_____

_____

Name

. . . .

You will need: plain pencil, coloured pencils

Mirror dance

Can you make up a dance together that would look like somebody dancing in front of a mirror? You can be the dancer and your friend can be your mirror image. Then swap over. Your movements have to be planned out and you must copy each other exactly. Show your dance to the class. Use the sheet to make some notes. It will help you remember the order of the movements in the dance.

Name

. . . .

You will need: plain pencil

Making up with my friends

How would you feel if you fell out with your best friend?

_____

_____

Write words to describe your feelings in the rain clouds. Draw some more clouds if you need to.

Name

. . . .

You will need: plain pencil

Making up with my friends

Can you think of any ways to make up with your friend?

Write your ideas in the suns below or along the rays. Draw some more suns if you need to.

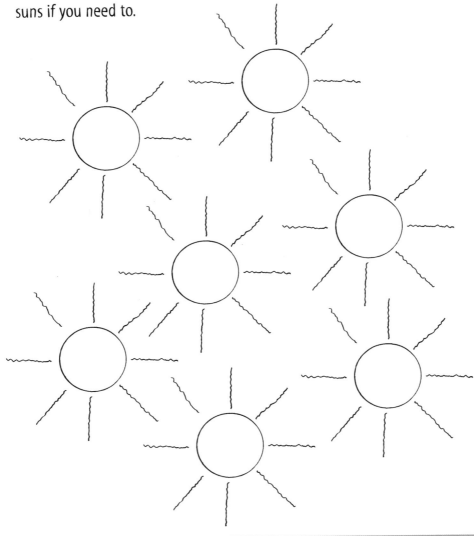

Name

. . . .

You will need: plain pencil

Friendship poem

Make up a friendship poem or dance. Show it to your friend and practise it together.

_____

_____

_____

_____

_____

_____

_____

_____

_____

_____

Name

. . . .

You will need: plain pencil

Hearts

Give people you love or care for a heart. Write inside the heart why you love them or care for them. Decorate the hearts. Cut them out and hand them to the people you love.

Draw more hearts if you need to.

To.............................
I love you because

....

....

To.............................
I love you because

....

....

How would you feel if someone gave you a heart?

_____

_____

Name

. . . .

You will need: plain pencil, coloured pencils, scissors

Special person award 1

Who would you choose to give this medal to? Choose someone special, write their name on the medal. Finish decorating it by colouring or painting it and then cut it out. Stick a piece of ribbon onto the back of the medal and hang it around the neck of your special person.

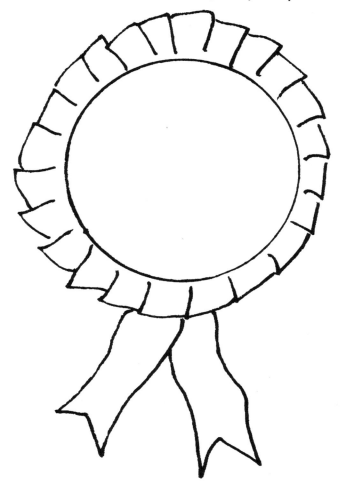

Name

. . . .

You will need: plain pencil, coloured pencils or paints, sticky tape, ribbon

Special person award 2

Who would you choose to give this certificate to? Choose someone special, write their name on the certificate. Finish decorating it by colouring or painting it and then cut it out. Roll up the certificate and tie it with a ribbon, then present it to that special person.

Certificate of Merit

The Special Person

This certificate is presented to ....
for caring about me and loving me.

Signed..............................

Name

. . . .

You will need: plain pencil, coloured pencils or scissors, ribbon

My Dreams and Wishes

Teacher notes

The focus in this section is back with the child again, this time helping them use and learn about their imagination. This pack contains worksheets in two sections. The first section, **Worksheet 1 – Dream collage** to **Worksheet 7 – Future** is as previous sections. The activity sheets are in a suggested order but the pick and mix option is also possible. The second section **Worksheet 8 – Space capsule** to **Worksheet 13 – Dreams can come true** should be completed in order from start to finish as it involves taking the child on an imaginary adventure.

This section of the resource is designed to help the children feel good about their own creativity and enjoy the extent of their imaginations. The child should know that it's perfectly normal to dream and have wishes, but the section also helps them realise that some dreams are achievable if they break them down into smaller manageable steps.

Worksheet 1 – Dream collage

Some discussion will need to take place before and after this worksheet. The children need to know and identify their own dreams. They may not realise they have any dreams but once they get started there will be no stopping them. Once the collage is complete, each child should then have an opportunity to show and share their collage with others, describing and explaining their choice of pictures and their related dreams.

Worksheet 2 and 3 – Zippy zappy zoom

These worksheets will help pupils use their imagination and think about what they would wish for themselves. The worksheets tap into their capacity for magical thinking. The children can choose which magic person they would like to have as their friend. The influence of Harry Potter and Hogwarts School may make the wizard more popular! Many children will be financially motivated here and wish for money. Remind them of other areas – they could wish for sunny days, happy holidays and good friends. In **Worksheet 3 – Zippy zappy zoom** pupils are encouraged to think of people they care about and imagine what they would like to conjure up for them. This will help pupils develop a capacity for empathy because they need to imagine not only what they might like to 'magic' for the person, but also to think about what that person would wish for themselves.

Circle Time suggestion

"I wish I could…" or "I dream of…"

Worksheet 4 – Hurray for our heroine/hero

These worksheets are for the boys and girls to design their own 'front cover' of a book which is all about them. Too often our culture encourages us to think only of heroes. This is created so that the expectations of 'heroism' are clear to both genders from an early age. In a class session you can ask children to name heroes and heroines they know or have heard of. These characters become important models for young children demonstrating what it is possible for people to achieve.

Worksheet 5 – Achievement tower

A class achievement tower can be built by cutting out the boxes with each child's achievement from the worksheet and creating a wall display. Extra turrets, flags, drawbridges and so on. can be added to make it more like a castle.

This activity can be repeated to encourage the children to set their own goals, making it progressively more difficult. You can also discuss a bigger goal, which will take longer to achieve. The time limit would need to be extended to three days, a week etc. Don't let the child make the goals too big or the time limit too great or they will never achieve it.

Worksheet 6 – Queen for a day / King for a day

These worksheets are for both genders. There is no reason why a girl cannot choose to be a King for a day or a boy a Queen. In class discussions you can explore what they imagine the differences are between what a King would do during a day and what a Queen would do. This can be extended into a discussion about why women might do different activities to a man. If there is a clear preference for one or the other the discussion can be expanded into exploring this too. Make sure that you affirm every child's choice. The class could talk about how it would feel to be their chosen person. What sort of things did you do in that day? Was it all good fun or were there some tasks which you hadn't realised or anticipated? What do they think the Queen of England does in a day? What do they think a historical figure such as King Charles II might have done (or any other relevant king figure that the pupils are aware of)?

Worksheet 7 – Future

This is quite a challenging task for young children. However, starting to think about themselves as they might be in the future begins to develop their 'intentionality.' This means their ability to focus on a goal in the future and work steadily for it. In order to do that, pupils need to be able to envisage what their goal will look like.

There is a second aim in this activity and that is to help children recognise their physical connection with their relatives. Children who have not got living relatives or who do not know what their blood relatives might look like can be encouraged to imagine what they themselves would like to look like in the future. They can think about older people they know. What are the signs of someone who is older? What is different about them? What is the same as younger people? This develops a pupil's capacity to observe as well as imagine.

The worksheet then expands the activity into thinking about the wider implications of being older and introduces the idea of thinking ahead and choosing what your interests could be or where you might live. This can be discussed in class and holidays can be remembered, thinking about whether those locations would be a good place to live and work. The lesson can incorporate a developing awareness of other cultures and of a wide variety of jobs and hobbies.

The following three worksheets form a series of activities each building on the preceding one.

Worksheet 8 – Space capsule

This worksheet taps into the children's wish to be all powerful and gives them permission to use their imagination when they have a spaceship to command.

Again the activity encourages children to put their dreams, wishes, fantasies and imagination into a more concrete form, for instance through words, writing and drawing. This begins to train children how to go about making their wishes come true. It also gives them permission to be as creative and imaginative as they can be without any judgements being made on what they produce.

Suggestion

■ The teacher can change the idea of space travel to a magic carpet to take you all over the world, or a time machine to take you into the future or back to the past. The following sheets would also have to be adapted using the different imagery.

Worksheet 9 – Blast off!

In this worksheet the children have another opportunity to climb into their friendly spaceship. This time they are going to go to another planet. Let the children's imaginations run riot. They can design new equipment for their spaceship if they need to. They can call on their memories of films they have seen or videogames they might play to give them ideas. Encourage them to put their own ideas and creations in and not just reproduce what they have seen.

This is a good topic for discussion and can lead to talk about the likelihood of extraterrestrial life for example. This could also incorporate ideas on multi-culturalism and appreciation of diversity, encouraging children to think 'outside the box' about ways people or other living beings could be different and interesting.

Suggestion

■ A large scale class model could be made and a play corner set up. Creative role play could then be encouraged with all kinds of dressing up clothes added – astronauts, extra terrestrial, walkie-talkies, breathing apparatus etc.

Worksheet 10 – The invitations

This worksheet extends the activity again and begins to include other people in the child's journey. Once they have travelled to one planet in their imagination they can then invite two friends to come with them to another.

Again they can be encouraged to think about what they might want to change in their spaceship to make sure they will all be able to travel safely and in comfort.

The worksheet asks them to fill in the invitations to two friends. These may be children in the class or they can be from the child's family or other friends ourside school. This exercise helps the children articulate who they would want with them and why. Where it is possible, encourage the child to actually give their friends their invitation. They can also take the invitations home with them and give them to friends outside the class.

In the classroom they can work in small groups, taking turns to describe:

- The planet they would visit
- The friends they would take and why
- The changes they might make in their spaceships

Suggestion

- After completing the invitations worksheet some additional activities can involve developing the notion of the undiscovered planet. Using some atmospheric music for stimulus the children can paint the planet. Encourage the children to think about what they hear and smell, not just what they see. This will help them make it a very much more realistic experience. They can talk about this in the class. What smell would they expect another planet to have? It can be anything – raspberry, flowers, rotten eggs etc.

- To have the children involved in a dramatisation of the exercise can make it an exciting project. For example, the class can use a variety of pitched or unpitched percussion and their voices to describe the planet and its atmosphere.

- The children can write a script describing what an intrepid group of three friends find when they get there. They can use the instruments to convey the atmosphere of what they feel and what they find at different points. The 'concept music' can be taped and listened to afterwards so the children can make comments.

- Some drama work is also possible. Working in pairs or groups the children should decide what would be discovered when they explore their planet. The creative music already taped can be used to add atmosphere and stimulus. Each group can perform their explorations to the class.

Worksheet 11 – Bravery badges

This is the last activity that is linked to the spaceship journeys. Once the children have flown their spaceships to an unknown planet and then gone to another one with their friends, they certainly deserve a bravery badge. This can be done at the end of the last activity or on the next occasion you have a session to help develop their self-esteem/emotional literacy.

In this activity they will make their own badge, choosing the one they prefer, colouring it in to make it uniquely theirs and then making it into a wearable badge by pasting it onto cardboard and using a safety pin to attach it to their clothes. This will help them feel pride in their imaginations and their willingness to have an adventure. You can draw their attention to how different the badges are, showing how unique each person is. This discussion can be expanded into other times they have been brave and when they have felt proud of themselves. This all helps to build self-esteem and self-awareness.

Worksheet 12 – The silver casket

This worksheet helps children use their imaginations to visualise, hear and feel their hopes and dreams. Imagining them in a box that they can open and close, look at and put away again, gives them a sense of power. The worksheet asks the children to write them all down so they again have practice at naming and clarifying their dreams and wishes. This can be an exercise that children share with one another after they have written them down. This can be done in small groups, as part of a classroom discussion, or in Circle Time.

Worksheet 13 – Dreams can come true

The children all need help to realise some dreams are achievable. Help them to break down the large dream to small achievable goals. Discuss how this can be done and how they can help each other to do this or help each other to achieve a task by one person doing one part of it and another person doing another.

When we are working towards a goal as adults a good strategy is to keep your vision of your goal in mind and to 'look' at it frequently. The last part of the activity gives this suggestion to the children and begins to teach them how to use their imaginations to help them achieve their dreams.

My dreams and wishes – pupil evaluation

Name .... Age .... Date ..../......./..........

Did I enjoy doing the sheet and having the discussion?

😃 Yes, very much   😐 It was OK   🙁 No, not at all

Worksheet

Dream collage	
Zippy zappy zoom 1	
Zippy zappy zoom 2	
Hurray for our heroine / hero	
Achievement tower	
Queen for the day King for the day	
Future	

Worksheet

Space capsule	
Blast off!	
The invitations	
Bravery badges	
The silver casket	
Dreams can come true	

You will need: plain pencil, coloured pencil

My dreams and wishes – teacher evaluation

Name .... Age .... Date ..../........../..............

How did the child cope with the sheet and participate in the discussion?

S – Satisfactory

WH – With help from teacher/friends

D – Had some difficulty

Worksheet	S	WH	D
1. Dream collage			
2. Zippy zappy zoom 1			
3. Zippy zappy zoom 2			
4. Hurray for my heroine / hero			
5. Achievement tower			
6. Queen for the day King for the day			
7. Future			
8. Space capsule			
9. Blast off!			
10. The invitations			
11. Bravery badges			
12. The silver casket			
13. Dreams can come true			

Dream collage

Cut out any pictures which make you think of your wishes. When you have a good selection, arrange them on this sheet, leaving no spaces showing through. When you are pleased with the arrangement, stick them into place.

Look at your collage when you feel sad or low and it will make you feel a lot better.

Name

. . . .

You will need: scissors, glue, selection of old magazines

Zippy zappy zoom 1

Fairy godmothers are people with magical powers. Imagine you could be granted three wishes for yourself by a fairy godmother.

What would they be?

Wish 1

_____

Wish 2

_____

Wish 3

_____

Draw one of your wishes here

Name

. . . .

You will need: plain pencil, coloured pencils

Zippy zappy zoom 1

Wizards are people with magical powers. Imagine you could be granted three wishes for yourself by a wizard.

What would they be?

Wish 1

_____

Wish 2

_____

Wish 3

_____

Draw one of your wishes here

Name

. . . .

You will need: plain pencil, coloured pencils

Zippy zappy zoom 2

The fairy godmother you have already met is very kind and she has allowed you to make three wishes for your friends or family. Who will you choose? What wish will you make for them?

Person 1   ☆☆☆☆☆

_____

Wish

_____

Person 2   ☆☆☆☆☆

_____

Wish

_____

Person 3   ☆☆☆☆☆

_____

Wish

_____

Name
. . . .
You will need: plain pencil

My Dreams and Wishes – Worksheet 3

Zippy zappy zoom 2

The wizard you have already met is very kind and he has allowed you to make three wishes for your friends or family. Who will you choose? What wish will you make for them?

Person 1

Wish

Person 2

Wish

Person 3

Wish

Name

. . . .

You will need: plain pencil

Hurray for our heroine

Imagine that you are the heroine of a book or a comic. Draw yourself on the front cover and give your book a title.

Book Title...

Name

. . . .

You will need: plain pencil, coloured pencils

Hurray for our hero

Imagine that you are the hero of a book or a comic. Draw yourself on the front cover and give your book a title.

Book Title..

Name
. . . .
You will need: plain pencil, coloured pencils

Achievement tower

Think carefully about what you can manage to achieve in one day. Fill in the box at the bottom of the achievement tower by writing in your idea. It may be about school or about home. It may be big, like remembering to say only kind things to people, or small, like remembering to hang up your coat.

At the end of the day, when you have achieved your goal, colour in the tower. You can cut it out and paste it onto cardboard and hang it up in a place where everyone can see it.

I can achieve _____

_____ by the end of the day.

Name

. . . .

You will need: plain pencil, coloured pencils, scissors, glue, cardboard

Queen for a day

Just try to imagine what it would be like to swap places with somebody for a day. It could be anyone at all – a pop star, a sports person, or maybe someone who isn't famous.

I'll swap with _____

Because _____

_____

Draw yourself during that day

Name
. . . .
You will need: plain pencil, coloured pencils

King for a day

Just try to imagine what it would be like to swap places with somebody for a day. It could be anyone at all – a pop star, a sports person, or maybe someone who isn't famous.

I'll swap with _____

Because _____

_____

Draw yourself during that day

Name

....

You will need: plain pencil, coloured pencils

My Dreams and Wishes – Worksheet 6

Future

Pick up the mirror and look closely at your own face. Do you look like an older member of your family? What will you look like when you're older? Think about when you are a parent or even a grandparent. Draw a portrait of yourself as you imagine you will look in the future.

Where will you live?

What job will you have?

What hobbies will you have?

Name
. . . .
You will need: plain pencil, coloured pencils, a mirror

Space capsule

It's a beautiful day and you are out for a walk when you come across an abandoned spaceship. You are very curious and decide to enter it. The spaceship starts up and asks you where you want to go. Fortunately, the ship is voice controlled and understands your commands.

Where would you go?

I would visit

_____

_____

Because

_____

Draw a picture of where you will go.

Name

. . . .

You will need: plain pencil, coloured pencils

Blast off!

Imagine going into a rocket and making an exciting trip all the way to an undiscovered planet – a place where no one has been before.

Finish drawing your rocket with you in it.

Name

. . . .

You will need: plain pencil, coloured pencil

The invitations

You are able to invite two people to go with you on your travels. Fill out these invitations and ask your crew to join you.

Trip of a Lifetime

To

I request the pleasure of your company to go to an undiscovered planet

Date _____ Time _____

You were chosen because _____

_____

Dream Come True

To

You are invited to join me on my journey to an undiscovered planet

Date _____ Time _____

I chose you because _____

_____

Name

. . . .

You will need: plain pencil, coloured pencil

Bravery badges

Choose a badge to decorate and colour. Cut it out and glue it onto some card. When it's dry, cut it out carefully. Tape the safety pin onto the back and wear it with pride.

Name

. . . .

You will need: plain pencil, coloured pencils, card, glue, scissors, safety pin, sticky tape

The silver casket

One rainy day you decide to play in your bedroom. Hunting for one of your games you open the cupboard door and looking into the corner you see the glint of a shiny object – it is a silver casket.

You open it up and inside you are amazed to find all of your dreams and wishes. Take time to look and enjoy yourself as you watch them.

Write them all down here

_____

_____

_____

_____

_____

_____

_____

_____

_____

_____

Name

. . . .

You will need: plain pencil

Dreams can come true

Shut the silver casket and keep your dreams safe. Every time you open it there will be more dreams.

Write about one dream and then write down what you will have to do to make it come true.

My dream

_____

_____

_____

To make my dream come true I will

_____

_____

_____

_____

_____

Remember when you feel sad or low take out the silver casket and look at your dreams. Think about which one you could make come true today.

Name
. . . .
You will need: plain pencil, coloured pencil

Daily Dilemmas

Teacher notes

All of these worksheets try to stretch the pupils to think about situations that are not clear cut with 'right' and 'wrong' answers. It involves them being empathic and thinking about how other people might feel and then finding a way to deal with the situation. This might mean they say what they feel and want very forcefully or very assertively. It may mean they say nothing because they don't want to upset anyone else. Or it may mean they find a way to negotiate. So much depends on the child and their experiences. These are rich discussions to hold with a class. Remember not to imply judgement or criticisms to the ideas they put forward. The point here is to debate and explore and then they can make up their own minds about what would be right for them.

Worksheet 1 – Happy at school

In this worksheet the pupils are asked to think about quite a complex set of problems. It requires them to be attuned to their own feelings (or imagined feelings) about hearing such life changing news. It also requires them to think about other people's responses to the same news. This is a worksheet that can be used in small groups or in a large classroom group and then discussed. It is important that they do not experience any judgement from you about their feelings on hearing the news. Use this opportunity to help them find a range of feeling words to describe what they might feel and remind them that they may feel quite contradictory feelings at times – one minute sad to go, the next angry and then the next quite excited. The question about whom they may talk to about this helps them explore how they would handle such a dilemma. Be aware that each child with their different personalities will have different strategies. Introvert children will want to think and feel their way through this on their own first, then they would talk to someone else. Extrovert children will want to talk it through immediately and work their way through their responses with other people first, and then they may think about it on their own later. Neither strategy is better than the other and each rests on self-knowledge on the part of the child. Asking the whole class to discuss the final part where they can explore ways to make the best of the forthcoming move will help children who have never come across this situation before. They will hear from pupils who have moved before and learn from them. The pupils who have been used to moving around will also have a chance to learn from pupils who have been used to one situation.

Worksheet 2 – Horrible haircut

In this worksheet the pupils are asked to explore themselves to decide how they would handle an embarrassing situation. Again, there is no right or wrong to this. Pupils must feel free to say what they think or to recount what they actually did if they have had a situation like that. Encourage pupils who have experienced something similar to talk about it and think whether they would do something different on another occasion. What is the learning for them? This helps children learn that looking back and reflecting on experiences as well as imagining them can be useful.

Worksheet 3 – Lost fare

This worksheet is about honesty and keeping yourself safe. It is quite hard for children to separate both elements of the scenario. When you have a discussion in the classroom about this, try to bring the two issues out and ask children what they think about each part. Find out if they would tell an adult about losing their fare if they were asked, or would they volunteer the information? Again, finding out if anyone has experienced this before and what they did will help pupils learn that every time we have a difficult event to deal with we can learn from it.

Worksheet 4 – Gangs

Underlying this worksheet is the knowledge that it can be helpful to write down the points for and against certain actions. There are different ways of handling this kind of exercise in the classroom. The pupils may each fill this in individually then have a classroom discussion, or the pupils could work in pairs or small groups and discuss together, ending with a review from each group. The maturity and sophistication of your class will dictate which format will work best. If you are not sure, try the individual filling in then class discussion first, as this method is easier to manage.

Worksheet 5 – No celebration cheer

In this worksheet 'illness and sadness' versus 'life goes on' are to be debated. In some cases it will depend on how the child feels about their uncle. In others it will be about how excited they are by the celebrations around them. This can be discussed together. It also incorporates a question about how they might manage or regulate their own emotions. As in some of the other sections of this resource, the point here is to help children develop their emotional literacy and through that, learn how to feel better about themselves.

Worksheet 6 – Sleepover

This worksheet explores how comfortable pupils are with expressing their fear and need for comfort, protection and reassurance. This is quite profound as it touches on whether they feel strong enough to be vulnerable. It also gives them another chance to learn about different ways to handle situations like this. Hearing other children talk about their ideas and experiences can give them many pointers for the future.

Worksheet 7 – Favourite things

This worksheet gets pupils working with one another and using their knowledge about logging information to show what they have found. The point about this activity is to demonstrate that people are the same in some ways and different in some ways and that this is a natural, human way to be. Discussions can move on to talking about how sometimes people don't act like that and what can be done when that happens. For instance, making sure everybody knows that 'people are different' and that everyone brings their own unique gifts and differences to the world.

Worksheet 8 – *Neighbours* v *Eastenders*

This worksheet helps children think creatively and effectively about possible solutions to conflicts. It is not a whole conflict resolution plan but picks up on part of the process and starts pupils practising the skills involved. It then helps pupils work in pairs or small groups to enact and rehearse some possible options. Discussions in the classroom can move into talking about other conflict resolutions they have been involved in and what happened in them. What worked? What didn't?

Worksheet 9 – Tea-time

This worksheet helps pupils think about how they can deal with situations where they come up against a big difference between them and a friend. There are different aspects to this as there will be emotions to come to terms with, and some decisions about what to do or not do. Does it matter? Can it be left? Who can they turn to? This activity can be conducted by you, using the sheet as a prompt and leading the class discussion through it, rather than the pupils working through it themselves.

Worksheet 10 – Show-off

This worksheet stretches a child to imagine themselves in another child's shoes. What would it be like to be a show-off and what would they do about someone acting like this? This worksheet helps you have a discussion about who has come across someone like this before. If anyone is honest enough they may be willing to talk about a time when they were a show-off. They could learn that most people show off some of the time. They could think about what the difference is between showing off and being proud of yourself. You can use this sheet as a prompt for class discussion, or hand it out for pupils to work through themselves and do a summarising session at the end, after a short time spent with several volunteers reading out what they have written.

Worksheet 11 – On top of the world

This exercise helps children recognise that they can have very complex and very conflicting emotions in one day. It focuses first on the feelings and then on what the child can do about it, if anything. The debates can take place between pupils. See if some take a strong stand on one side and some strongly think another. Ask them to set up a debating session on it. The rest of the class can then comment on whether the situation can be reduced to a right way and a wrong way to look at it. Make sure that no criticism or judgement is implied in this commentary.

Worksheet 12 – Florida photos

This worksheet focuses on feelings again and encourages pupils to think about themselves in an upsetting situation. The subtext of this worksheet is to help children rehearse how they can help themselves when they have a disaster like that with precious things. The class can take turns talking about what they have written while you manage any discussion around what they have said.

Worksheet 13 – Sticks and stones

This worksheet touches on bullying and how pupils might handle a situation that begins to feel like they are being victimised. It focuses on them and their feelings. It opens up discussion about times when this kind of thing might have happened to anyone in the class. For this sort of disclosure the level of trust and openness has to be very high and your management of the climate in the room will be very important. Being gentle, empathic and respectful will help this happen and allow the children to explore this topic in a useful way.

Worksheet 14 – Make your dreams come true

This is another worksheet that helps pupils think about their feelings and (mentally at least) rehearse their possible actions. This is a good activity to have pupils do in small groups or pairs and work through together. You can orchestrate a discussion when they finish each section in the worksheet.

Worksheet 15 – Being left out

This worksheet touches on a very painful experience that a child might have. Being left out is a hard situation to support yourself through. Whole class discussions are 'safer' to talk in than more private ones with small groups. If the class is a bit reluctant to pick up this topic ask them to talk about people they know who have been left out in some way and how they might have felt and what they did. This is a tender subject and may need you to approach it obliquely.

Worksheet 16 – Reach your target

This is not so much a dilemma as a self-management topic, which is an important aspect of self-esteem and emotional literacy. You can start this exercise by asking the pupils about the times they have not managed to complete a target. From then they can go on to complete the sheet. Younger children will need help through each part. Discussion can be held either throughout or at the end.

Worksheet 17 – Good friends

This is about loyalty and conflicting responsibilities. Again, the worksheet brings out important and complex issues. The best way to conduct this activity is to use the sheet as a prompt and read through it, giving examples and encouraging the children to talk about their experiences. It also asks children to think about friendship and what makes a good friend. Allowing the children to think this through without criticism or judgement is very important, as they will all have different views on this. And as we know, difference is interesting and exciting!

Daily dilemmas – pupil evaluation

Name .... Age .... Date ..../......./...........

Did I enjoy doing the sheet and having the discussion?

Yes, very much   It was OK   No, not at all

Worksheet

Happy at school	
Horrible haircut	
Last fare	
Gangs	
No celebration cheer	
Sleepover	
Favourite things	
Neighbours v *Eastenders*	
Tea-time	

Worksheet

Show-off	
On top of the world	
Florida photos	
Sticks and stones	
Make your dreams come true	
Being left out	
Reach your target	
Good friends	

You will need: plain pencil, coloured pencil

Daily dilemmas – teacher evaluation

Name .... Age .... Date ..../........./...........

How did the child cope with the sheet and participate in the discussion?

S – Satisfactory   WH – With help from teacher/friends   D – Had some difficulty

Worksheet	S	WH	D
1. Happy at school			
2. Horrible haircut			
3. Last fare			
4. Gangs			
5. No celebration cheer			
6. Sleepover			
7. Favourite things			
8. *Neighbours* v *Eastenders*			
9. Tea-time			
10. Show-off			
11. On top of the world			
12. Florida photos			
13. Sticks and stones			
14. Dreams can come true			
15. Being left out			
16. Reach your target			
17. Good friends			

Happy at school

You're in primary year 5 and very happy at school. You get on well with your teacher and are working well in class. Your friends are brilliant and you've known some of them since nursery. One tea-time you learn that you have to move to another town. This means moving to a new house and changing schools.

You don't want to spoil things for any important people in your life, but you don't want to move.

How do you feel?

_____

_____

Do you tell someone how you feel?

_____

_____

What do your friends say when you let them know?

_____

_____

How can you make the best of the move?

_____

_____

Name

. . . .

You will need: plain pencil

Horrible haircut

You've decided to spend more than you normally would on a new haircut and you went to the trendiest hairdressers in town. You've shown off about where you're going and how much it's going to cost for days. However, things don't go as planned and you absolutely hate your new haircut.

How do you face your friends the next day?

_____

_____

Do you lie and pretend your hairstyle is very modern?

_____

Would you wear a hat or try to go to another hairdressers to re-style your hair?

_____

Maybe you could just be very brave and stand up to all the laughing and jeering. How would you feel?

_____

_____

Would you show off the next time you visit the hairdresser?
Why? / Why not?

_____

Name
. . . .
You will need: plain pencil

Lost Fare

Normally you catch the bus to get to school but today you lost your bus fare so you couldn't get on the bus.

What do you do?

_____

_____

_____

How do you get to school?

_____

_____

_____

Do you own up and admit you lost the fare?

_____

_____

_____

Name

. . . .

You will need: plain pencil

Gangs

You really want to be part of a new group of friends who you really admire. They have the newest, trendiest gear and seem so cool. You're really pleased because they let you walk to school with them, but they take a detour to the shops. They tell you to steal something from one of the shops and then they'll let you be part of the gang.

What would you do? You'll be late for school if you take too long to decide, and you'll get a punishment exercise if you are late as this has happened before.

Write down two lists under each heading

1. What would be good
about joining the gang

2. What would be bad
about joining the gang

_____ _____

_____ _____

_____ _____

_____ _____

_____ _____

_____ _____

_____ _____

Name

. . . .

You will need: plain pencil

No celebration cheer

Religious festivals and celebrations can mean a good time for many people. There are school holidays, perhaps presents and parties, fun films on TV, good food and treats. You love it. This year your uncle is very ill and the celebrations have been cancelled.

How do you feel?

_____

_____

You have a choice that you can go ahead and enjoy your own school parties, but you feel bad. How do you feel when you're out celebrating and enjoying yourself and your uncle is very ill and other people are worrying about him?

_____

_____

What could you do to help yourself feel better?

_____

_____

What could you do to help the people who are worrying?

_____

Name

. . . .

You will need: plain pencil

Sleepover

During a sleepover party at your friend's house there's a very bad thunderstorm. When you're at home, you would be terrified and you've even crept into someone else's bed on similar occasions. The storm is loud and you feel frightened.

1. Do you let your friends know your fear?

_____

_____

2. Do you speak to an adult in the house?

_____

_____

3. What will your friends say about you being scared in a storm?

_____

_____

4. What do you say when you return home the next morning?

_____

_____

_____

Name

. . . .

You will need: plain pencil

Favourite things

You and your friend should make up a questionnaire to discover at least 10 favourite things about other classmates. Gather together all your information and display it. Your display should be neat, clear and easy to understand. Here are some suggestions — a table of results using tally marks e.g. favourite colour

Green	II	2
Yellow	⊬⊬II	7
Red	III	3

A tally chart

A pie chart – favourite colour

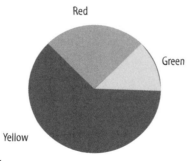

A bar graph – favourite colour

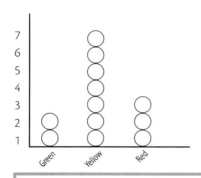

Remember, everyone is different and likes different things.

Name

. . . .

You will need: plain pencil

Neighbours v Eastenders

You and your brother are arguing over the TV. Your favourite programme is on another channel but it is on at the same time as your brother's favourite. How do you solve this argument? Here are some suggestions. Add some of your own.

1. Is there another TV in the house?

2. Can you toss a coin?

3. Agree to watch half of one programme followed by half of the other.

4. Watch one programme one week and another the next week.

5. _____

6. _____

7. _____

8. _____

9. _____

10. _____

Find a partner or make a group and act out the situation and some of the solutions.

_____

Name

. . . .

You will need: plain pencil

Tea-time

Some friends are coming for tea at your house. You ask them what their favourite tea would be. They choose one that you hate! Do you complain or do you keep quiet?

Explain why

_____

_____

_____

How do you feel once you've made your decision?

_____

_____

What will happen once they have left? Who will you talk to?

_____

_____

_____

What do you think they will say? What will you say?

_____

_____

Name

. . . .

You will need: plain pencil

Show-off

A new person has joined your class and they're a bit of a show-off. They're always telling you how their house is bigger than yours, their clothes are more fashionable than yours and they're on the football team and you're not.

1. How does this make you feel?

_____

_____

_____

2. Why do you think they behave like this?

_____

_____

_____

3. What are you going to do to stop it happening?

_____

_____

_____

Name

. . . .

You will need: plain pencil

On top of the world

It's your birthday, you got what you wanted and you're having a party tonight. At school you've got some test results back and you've done very well. It's a great day and you're feeling on top of the world. One of your friends is jealous about your birthday present and starts to spoil your special day by talking behind your back and being nasty.

How do you feel?

_____

_____

_____

In what ways does it change the day you're having?

_____

_____

_____

What could you do about it?

_____

_____

_____

Name

. . . .

You will need: plain pencil

Florida photos

Last summer you went to Disneyland, Florida, the place you've wanted to visit for ages. You had a brilliant time and the photos are a good memory of the times you had. You often take them out and browse through them. You keep them in a box next to the immersion heater. The plumbing is being renewed and there has been an accident with the photos. They've been damaged by water and completely ruined.

1. How do you feel looking through your own photos of happy times?

_____

_____

_____

2. How do you feel when you see the damaged photos?

_____

_____

_____

3. What can you do to help keep the memories of the special times alive in your head and heart?

_____

_____

_____

Name

. . . .

You will need: plain pencil

Sticks and stones

In the park a group of people who you normally play with start to gang up on you and call you horrible names. You haven't done anything to deserve this and you don't know why they're behaving in such a nasty way towards you.

1. Do you try to stop them? Ask them why? Or do you just leave?

_____

_____

_____

2. How do you feel?

_____

_____

_____

3. How will you feel when you have to face them again?

_____

_____

_____

Name
. . . .
You will need: plain pencil

Make your dreams come true

Your teacher has asked you to write down all the dreams and wishes you have for yourself, your family and your friends.

The person next to you laughs at them. They tell you they're silly because they will never happen and never come true.

1. How do you feel when this person makes fun of you?

_____

_____

2. What could you say to them?

_____

_____

3. Do you feel strong enough to stand up for yourself or would you need some help from an adult?

_____

_____

4. Who could help you?

_____

_____

_____

Name
. . . .
You will need: plain pencil

Being left out

Everyone in your group of friends has been invited to a friend's birthday treat day out, apart from you.

1. Do you ask why you weren't invited?

_____

_____

_____

2. How does it feel to be left out?

_____

_____

_____

3. How can you make yourself feel better? List some ideas.

_____

_____

_____

_____

Name

. . . .

You will need: plain pencil

Reach your target

You've set yourself a target – something you want to achieve by the end of the week. But somehow you didn't manage to reach your target.

How do you feel about not achieving your target?

If you feel bad about it, don't worry. Reassure yourself that you can achieve it next time. What could you do to help yourself achieve this target the next time? Here are some ideas.

- Give yourself longer – two weeks for example

- Promise yourself a reward when you achieve the target

- Break down the target to smaller mini-targets to achieve after two or three days

Can you add more?

_____

_____

Set yourself a target now. Make it small.

_____

_____

Name

. . . .

You will need: plain pencil

Good friends

Emma's best friend is called David. They do everything together including walking to school together. They know they must walk together and they must be at school for nine o'clock. One day Emma asks David to go to the park and play on the swings. David knows this will make them late for school but he also knows he should walk with Emma to school.

1. What should he do?

_____

_____

2. What would you do?

_____

_____

3. Think about being a good friend. What does it mean to be a good friend?

_____

_____

Name

. . . .

You will need: plain pencil

Bibliography

Armstrong, T. (1999) *7 Kinds of Smart*, Plume Publishing.

Borba, M. (1989) *Esteem Builders: A Teacher/Counsellor Guide*, Jalmar Press.

Canfield, J. & Wells, H. (1993) *100 Ways to Enhance Self-Concept in the Classroom*, Allyn & Bacon.

Collins, M. (1997) *Keep Yourself Safe*, Lucky Duck Publishing.

Gardner, H. (1993) *Frames of Mind*, Basic Books Publishing.

Gottman, J. & Declaire J. (1998) *Raising an Emotionally Intelligent Child*, Fireside Books

Illsley Clarke, J. (1978) *Self Esteem: A Family Affair*, Hazelden.

Mruk, C. *Self-Esteem: Research, Theory and Practice*, Springer Publishing.

Rae, T. (1998) *Dealing with Feeling*, Lucky Duck Publishing.

Rudd, B. (1998) *Talking is for Kids*, Lucky Duck Publishing.

Sharp, P. (2001) *Nurturing Emotional Literacy*, David Fulton Publishing.

Wallace, F. & Caesar, D. (1998) *Not you Again*, Lucky Duck Publishing.

Wallace, F. (1998) *What else can I do with you?* Lucky Duck Publishing.